By the *Golden Quill A*
nominated author

YOU'LL
MANAGE

Lessons Learned From A Former CEO

*Thoughts on Entrepreneurism,
Business and Life*

Chris Allison

For Jane
Thanks for going to Jack's party.

ACKNOWLEDGEMENTS

Slightly different versions of many of these essays first appeared in the *Pittsburgh Quarterly*, so I would like to thank Doug Heuck, the editor and publisher of the magazine for granting permission to include them. I'd especially like to thank my editor, Ross Howell, who I call *The Magic Man* for reasons all too clear as you read more. I'd also like to thank my Mom and Dad for inspiring me through their example. And finally, I want to thank my wife, Janie, for making me a better man.

TABLE OF CONTENTS

PREFACE

I was a freshman in high school when the film *All The President's Men* was released in April 1976. One hundred and thirty-eight minutes later, I wanted to be a writer. More specifically, I wanted to be Bob Woodward.

So when I attended Allegheny College in the early '80s, I majored in English; took a lot of writing courses; wrote for the college's alumni publication, *Allegheny Magazine*; and worked as a stringer for the local daily, *The Meadville Tribune*.

A year after graduation, I took a job in the public relations business because that was as close to being a real writer as I could get. It was kind of a weird job. I did everything from promoting the local ballet company to writing new product announcements about gas masks.

My favorite *oeuvre* was a gripping article that I penned for *Pork '86* magazine, the journal of the hog-producing industry. I wove an intricate case-study yarn about dosimeter-tube usage in swine containment areas.

I'll bet you didn't know that pig flatulence is actually quite dangerous, so it must be monitored closely.

Unfortunately—actually, quite fortunately—for 16 years I was sidetracked from those literary heights to work at a tech company my Dad had founded. By accident I ended up becoming the company's CEO. I didn't trip. The original management team simply lost enthusiasm and left. My Dad was ill with diabetes and heart disease at the time, and needed to tend to his other company, which did heavy construction for the gas industry.

A few years later, with me at the helm, the tech company went public. In 2000, five years after the IPO, annual sales reached $114 million and the company was valued at $2 billion on the NASDAQ exchange. English major with pig pen creds. Go figure.

When I left the tech company job in 2005, I got a call from Doug Heuck, the former business editor of the *Pittsburgh Post-Gazette*. He was starting a new magazine called *Pittsburgh Quarterly* that would focus on business and the arts in our remade old steel town. He asked if I'd be interested in writing a column for *PQ* that he wanted to call, "You'll Manage."

Hence the title. The pieces that follow are largely the fruits of my labors for Doug, along with a few editorials I wrote for newspapers. Some of the articles here have never been published.

When I was in college, I had the good fortune to meet two great writers. One was my professor, the novelist-in-residence at Allegheny, Alfred Kern. Sadly, this wise and talented man passed away a few years ago. The other was the editor of *Allegheny Magazine*, Ross Howell, who fortunately is alive and well and helped me edit these essays. For his consent to steal away from his own work to sprinkle magic dust on these words I am extremely grateful.

Chris Allison
August 2013

FIVE MOMENTS

Every year, I look fore and aft with anticipation and nostalgia as I play George Bailey from *It's a Wonderful Life*. Most of us experience five moments in life that dictate how it will unfold. Of the five, maybe we're in control of one or two.

Remembering my five moments helps me understand that my life's glass is definitely half full. Because it's instructive to consider your moments, let me tell you mine as a means of providing guideposts. My moments follow chronologically, rather than in order of importance.

The Day I Almost Died

From the time that I was 12, I picked up extra cash by working at my Dad's heavy construction company in Erie. Basically, his company fixed holes in the streets made by the local gas company crews when they repaired leaks.

I loved the job. It was physical and out of doors. Because I didn't have a good enough eye to finish concrete or spread asphalt, I worked the dig-out crew, which meant I destroyed things. For eight hours a day, I'd break up the street with a jackhammer and remove the debris.

The day before 1978's Fourth of July, I thought I'd create some fireworks of my own. The compressor that powered the jackhammer ran out of gas.

As I was refilling it with a gas can and galvanized funnel, the compressor exploded. Flames engulfed my lower extremities. Despite my furiously rolling on the ground while my co-workers beat down the flames, the fire covering my legs just wasn't going out.

Luckily, we were working across the street from an industrial supply company which was having a sale on fire extinguishers on their front sidewalk. A store clerk leapt over the counter, grabbed a fire extinguisher and sprayed me with retardant. Had it not been for him, I probably would have died.

After a month in an isolation room, hot whirlpool baths, daily intramuscular injections of Demerol and an unrequited romance with a candy striper, I left the hospital.

I was never able to thank the man who saved my life because I never saw him again. There are angels among us and mine disappeared like morning mist on Lake Erie.

Meeting Jane and 0 for 19

Life moved along nicely. I graduated from Allegheny College and began working in the public relations business. At work one day I got a call from my Dad, who asked me to join his start-up technology company. He wanted to hire me to write brochures and news releases, and I agreed to his offer.

However, due to an accelerating lack of conviction among the other founders and managers, who pretty much disappeared, leaving my Dad in the lurch, I ended up managing the joint, while he tended to his other businesses.

Running an under-funded start-up company is, as Carol Burnett described childbirth, like "taking your lower lip and pulling it up over your forehead."

One Friday night I visited my Dad in the hospital after his second heart bypass surgery. I was flat-ass beat and told him I was thinking about skipping our banker's annual Christmas party that evening. As usual, my Dad was insistent and wise. "Chris," he said, "we owe this guy a lot of money. Go."

That night, I met Jane. A little more than a year later, I stood next to her while we exchanged vows. When we returned from our honeymoon, Jane told me a secret she'd been keeping.

"Chris, I found this lump on my breast," she said.

Two weeks later, Jane underwent a surgical procedure called a lumpectomy, which indicated she had cancer. A second procedure, called a lymph node dissection, followed.

This entailed removing lymph nodes from Jane's body and completing a biopsy of each to determine if any contained cancer. Like canaries in a coal mine, the lymph nodes would indicate danger. The more cancer-bearing lymph nodes found, the more the cancer had spread.

Fortunately, Jane had a hitting slump. She was 0 for 19. There was no cancer beyond the lump that was removed earlier. To this day, she wears a charm that I bought for her 20 years ago with the inscription, "0 for 19."

The Day I Lost My Dad

They say you don't really become a man until you lose your Dad. Six years after my promotion to CEO and our under-funded tech company's successful initial public offering, I grew up. One Sunday morning, I got a phone call from my brother Mike, a Catholic priest stationed in Erie.

"Get up here as soon as you can," Mike said. "He had a heart attack."

Mike's call followed an episode back in 1978, when my Dad had been rushed to the hospital for heart bypass surgery at the ripe old age of 37, and his second bypass, a few days before I met Jane at the Christmas party. He nearly died both times, but he'd managed to pull through.

This time was different. Five minutes after his first call, Mike rang back.

"Take your time," he said. "He's gone."

I'd never again see the man I devoted my life to making proud of me. I'd never again experience the bluster and humor of one of the purest entrepreneurs

I'd ever known. I'd never get another phone call in the middle of the night and listen to one of his ideas. I'd never again hold my side in pain after laughing at one of his jokes or funny turns of phrase.

"Don't confuse benevolence with stupidity," he'd say, or, "That guy doesn't have 20 years' experience. He has one year's experience 20 times."

In an instant, my hero was gone.

As CEO of the tech company, I traveled almost every week, meeting with customers. My Dad always wanted me to call him and report on my trip as I drove home from the airport. To this day, when I'm leaving Pittsburgh International for Ben Avon, I reflexively reach for my cell.

Turning Down the Deal

A year after my Dad died, I got a call from the CEO of a telecom "roll-up" being put together by a New York investment firm. A roll-up is a holding company consisting of a group of companies in the same industry.

The roll-up's CEO wanted to discuss, "How we might work together," which is financial industry code for, "We want to acquire your company." As our tech firm's CEO, I had a fiduciary responsibility to my shareholders to have a discussion with the roll-up's chief, despite telling him, "The company is not for sale." This also is financial industry code for, "How much money are you talking about?"

After a protracted mating period that concluded in December 1999, the roll-up's CEO presented an all-cash offer nicely higher than our current stock price, which had been mired in the $20 range for years. But there was a catch. We had to close the deal before reporting our quarterly earnings to Wall Street.

Our modest tech firm was having a monster quarter. Projected sales for 2000 looked even better. Our board took a collective deep breath, and we said, "No."

Within six months, we were doubling sales and our stock was trading at $300 per share. The rest, as they say, is history.

Running into Nej

Five tumultuous years later, after some guys decided to fly a couple of planes into the World Trade Center and the dot.com bubble burst, our tech company stayed profitable by sticking to our frugal knitting and buying a couple of companies ourselves. But I was, quite simply, burned out.

I remember walking home from church with Jane one Sunday after a long and demanding week with the business. She took my hand and said, "We aren't going to be doing this in five years, are we?"

Not long after Jane asked me that question, we went to a Pirates game. I noticed a guy sitting a row or two in front of us. He looked really familiar. I leaned forward and tapped him on the shoulder. "Brian?" I asked. Sure enough, it was my old classmate from Allegheny College, who everyone called "Nej."

For the next nine innings, Nej told me his story. He had started a tech company, sold it and decided to teach entrepreneurship at a faith-based college. As the Pirates' season progressed, he and I talked many times, mapping out a future of giving back.

Six months later, I announced my retirement from the tech company. It feels like a lifetime ago.

Those are my five moments. What are yours?

MOVING UP THE ENTREPRENEURIAL LADDER

Not long ago my heart sank when I read that our local metropolitan area ranked 48th among the 50 top cities in *Entrepreneur* magazine's list of the best cities for entrepreneurs. Some people might think making the top 50 is an accomplishment, but it's nowhere good enough.

Entrepreneurship is a Pittsburgh tradition and the life-blood of our future growth.

So how can we move up the entrepreneurial ladder? In my mind, we can create critical mass by addressing issues like seed funding, entrepreneurial education and harnessing the collective power of local economic development activities.

Water the Acorns

A lot of start-up executives will tell you that it's harder to raise $500,000 than it is to raise $2 million. But seed money is not as bountiful locally as it could be or should be.

For many venture capital firms, a minority of investments account for a majority of profits. They invest in risky ideas, so their batting averages are low. But when they hit the ball, it usually bounces into the river.

Because venture capital firms only can invest in companies with addressable markets exceeding $500 million, they usually don't make bets on companies that can only hit a single.

Seed money for small start-ups must come from high-net-worth individuals in the private sector, sometimes called "angels." Places like Palo Alto, Calif.; Boston, Mass.; Raleigh, N.C.; and Austin, Texas; have become hotbeds of technology.

Why? Because young tech-company founders, whose companies have grown into mighty financial oak trees, showered start-up capital on acorns that had fallen nearby, folks with good ideas. What's the reasoning behind these tech angels' decisions to invest? Partly, it's empathy for the start-up's plight; partly, it's wealth creation; most probably, it's the fun of doing it.

In Pittsburgh we need to create an environment where there are incentives for successful local entrepreneurs to reinvest their personal wealth in local start-ups. A nice complement to our state's venture capital program would be tax breaks for angel investors who deploy capital intrastate for start-ups or invest in venture capital firms based within state lines.

Teach Your Children Well

Most start-up tech companies don't fail because their leaders didn't work hard enough or didn't have good ideas. They fail primarily due to poor business planning. If more entrepreneurs understood market research techniques, long-term strategic planning, creating competitive differences, cash-flow planning, go-to-market strategies, capital formation techniques and basic management techniques, their companies would have a better fighting chance in the tech marketplace.

Entrepreneurial education on a high school, collegiate and executive seminar basis is a must. Every major university in our region has entrepreneurial education programs. Many are taught on a graduate and undergraduate level. Organizations such as the National Foundation for Teaching Entrepreneurship help high schools, often in low-income districts, to provide classes in business, finance and technology.

Why couldn't the Commonwealth of Pennsylvania create a program such as the Job Training Partnership Act to provide tuition dollars for this type of education for adult entrepreneurs? Why can't an introduction to entrepreneurship be part of a life skills curriculum that is mandated for high schools across the state?

Our Gang of Seven

We have a lot of community organizations that want to help local business creation. All are well-intentioned, with different charters and different goals. I wonder if they sometimes step on one another's toes? Human nature being what it is, maybe they even compete a bit with one another. Is there a way to make sure that their efforts are compounded and strengthened, not duplicated or stymied?

The Group of Eight (G8) is an international association that represents 65 percent of the world's economy and includes the United States, Canada, France, Germany, Italy, Japan, Russia and the United Kingdom. The leaders of these countries get together every year to find ways that they can work together to better our global economy.

Could we bring together the leaders of local economic development agencies to form a group that functions in a regional way, much the same as the international version?

What if the state gave this local group of leaders a chunk of its venture capital program dollars, with the proviso that the group hires a staff of experienced venture capitalists to administer the fund? After all, members do have day jobs running their own organizations. The profits of this venture fund would then be redeployed regionally in the form of economic development grants.

A portion of the profits also would be used to provide reasonable incentives for the pros running the fund. Good venture capitalists do not come cheaply.

Green Cards with Diplomas

Author Tom Friedman has argued that the world is flat. We need to think globally. You know how we beat China and India in the world economy? Technology and talent. I say we should take the advice of a highly successful local venture capitalist. The diploma any foreign student receives from a local college should have a green card stapled to it. How about we create a local bureau of immigration lawyers that provides free legal service to foreign kids coming out of local schools? If we get them a green card, they must commit to living in the region for another five years.

THE BIONIC
ENTREPRENEUR?

For me, fall marks not only the return of autumn leaves, cider and football, but also returning to my role as a college entrepreneurship instructor. Despite this being my third year teaching the subject, I'm still troubled by a gnawing, fundamental question: Can anyone actually teach someone to be an entrepreneur? Is start-up a trait you're born with, or can it be instilled through a well-considered pedagogy?

While the debate over nature vs. nurture, whether performance is genetic or learned, has raged for centuries, the study of entrepreneurism is relatively new. And it's on the rise. According to *Inc.* magazine, the number of universities offering entrepreneur courses has grown from 300 in the early 1980s to more than 1,600 today. Locally, students at Duquesne University can now major in Entrepreneurial Studies. Almost every regional college or university has at least one course on small business or entrepreneurism.

To seek the answer to my question of whether entreneurship can be taught, over the summer I traveled to Wellesley, Mass. This quaint New England town is home to the Mecca of entrepreneurial education in the U.S. and maybe the world: Babson College. Presiding over this kingdom of start-up thought is its all-knowing prophet Jeffry Timmons, author of the classic book, *New Venture Creation*, and creator of the famed "Timmons Model."

Along with 50 college professors and entrepreneurs, I attended a week-long seminar about teaching entrepreneurship. I figured if I couldn't find the answer to my question at Babson, I might as well end my quest for this philosophical grail.

My seminar classmates ranged from Blake and Dave, laid-back California surfer dudes who are also hard-nosed venture capitalists—to Mark from Arkansas, a somewhat cynical, yet erudite professor who teaches entrepreneurship while running a multimillion-dollar home restoration development company—to Wayne from Wyoming, who freaked me out because he sounds just like the actor who plays the shrink Emil Skoda in cable TV's *Law and Order*. In his Dr. Skoda voice, Wayne brought sober realism to every discussion because, in addition to teaching, he runs a start-up company.

While I tended to gravitate toward the entrepreneurs and investors who taught as a sideline, I realized that the more time I spent with full-time professional academics, the more I respected them. Good ones work at least 50 hours a week preparing for classes—three hours of prep for every hour of teaching—grading papers and meeting with students, which is where a lot of the learning takes place.

As soon as we "dropped the puck," to use Prof. Timmons' vernacular, we started exploring the source of entrepreneurism. Are people simply born with the Right Stuff or can they be trained to become the next Steve Jobs?

Speaker after speaker explained that a key to entrepreneurial performance is shedding managerial convention and bringing sanity to what is perceived as chaos. The goal is to be an anarchist in an orderly fashion.

Entrepreneurs must think outside the box about solutions to customer problems. They must make sure those solutions are unique in big and growing markets and can command prices that create high profit margins. Orderly anarchy can create open-mindedness to change, tension and conflict and an obsessive thirst for opportunity.

People used to call this process thinking on your feet, yet few corporate executives can do it for fear of stepping outside the lines of convention.

Entrepreneurs should constantly learn what customers want and then work as a team to give it to them. Entrepreneurs should not take a risk unless it's fully evaluated and promises a big payoff. Timmons' approach is like flying a fighter jet—high-speed and low drag. Above all, he says, entrepreneurs should have fun. If it ain't fun, why bother? Life is too short.

I agree with Timmons' approach. What do my fellow entrepreneurs-turned-academics think?

Some believe entrepreneurs are really leaders of a counter-culture movement in American business. Most people don't realize that Apple's Jobs and Steve Wozniak, Microsoft's Gates and Ballmer, and Michael Dell were pretty much hell-raisers in college. They worked on stuff that was "cool" to them, but also lucrative. This business radicalism wasn't born of a disrespect for authority. Entrepreneurs respect authority—their own and their customers'. And every time their customers give them a gripe, they think of how to fix a problem—provided there's money in it. Instead of burning down the administration building, they would be more apt to sell the college president a software program that minimizes paper and allows students to download textbooks and take tests online.

Most people think of entrepreneurs as frantic individuals—business hummingbirds who flit from idea to idea, sipping at possibilities until one seems to taste especially good. The key for teachers is helping entrepreneurs to be purposeful—turning them from hummingbirds into falcons, relentless in their sharp-eyed hunt for innovation and profit.

The professors believe entrepreneurial education is really about getting students to focus outward on customers, not inward on processes. They want students to understand that when customers buy a product or service from a company, they are essentially hiring the organization to do a job for them.

True success is finding unique ways to identify such jobs, opportunities that pay well in large and growing markets. It is not, as corporate lemmings seem to believe, attending pointless meetings, writing cover-your-bum e-mails and worrying about whether your cubicle neighbor is more politically astute than you are.

By the end of my week's quest, I felt I had found my answer. A chosen few are born with all the attributes of an entrepreneur, but even they must be disciplined and molded. Those without the full-blown start-up gene can be trained to add value to an entrepreneurial venture or make a big company more nimble.

Now I see my students in much the same way the Bob Fosse character played by Roy Scheider in the film *All That Jazz* viewed his. "I can't make you a great dancer," the character said. "I don't even know if I can make you a good dancer. But, if you keep trying and don't quit, I know I can make you a better dancer."

WHATEVER HAPPENED TO THE MAN IN THE GRAY FLANNEL SUIT?

In 1955 Sloan Wilson published his groundbreaking novel on the trials of corporate America in the 1950s. Telling the story of a young executive who works tirelessly in what would become known as the white-collar world, *The Man in the Gray Flannel Suit* also became a hit film in 1956 starring Gregory Peck and Jennifer Jones.

Wilson's protagonists are Tom and Betsy Rath, a couple struggling with tending their growing family in suburban obscurity. In the mid-'50s, the Rath character inspired many to become hard-working "company men."

Wearing the uniform of a dark suit, tie and always a fedora, the company man was a no-nonsense executive who analyzed problems, ran solutions up the flagpole, modernized production and followed the rules. Hard work and patrician values led to a happy life and a comfortable retirement with a well-earned pension.

Sound idyllic? Quaint? Certainly less complicated than today, right? Tom and Betsy Rath had it pretty good in hindsight. Or did they? What was it really like, living and doing business back then? Would Tom and Betsy recognize our world? Let's find out.

Debt and Taxes

Despite the fact that the cost of living was higher in the '50s, people didn't face the debt that looms today. In 1959, personal income was roughly twice the debt people carried. Figures from the Federal Reserve Bank of St. Louis show that American household debt, including consumer debt and mortgage loans, rose from 68 percent of disposable income in 1980 to 128 percent of income in 2007.

However, while they bore a lower personal debt load, workers in 1956 had to put in more hours to acquire goods than we do today. "[We work] 300 hours less than a man in the 1950s to pay for a family car," writes Stuart A. Kallen in his book, *A Cultural History of the United States Through the Decades: The 1950s*. Home ownership was also more costly. "A fifties worker worked 6.5 hours per square foot for his home," Kallen writes, "versus 5.6 hours per square foot [today]."

Of course, if you were rich in the 1950s, you weren't likely to be a happier camper, either. The income tax rate for the highest one percent of wage earners was 88 percent back then.

The Looming Menace

In the '50s, Americans were afraid of a Communist enemy that they did not understand. In October 1957, when the Soviet Union launched its basket-ball-sized *Sputnik I* into orbit, the earth's first artificial satellite didn't prompt celebration as a scientific advancement. Instead, *Sputnik I* sent waves of fear across the United States, as people realized that it could serve as a delivery system for a nuclear warhead. Elementary school teachers soon taught children to "duck and cover" under their desks during Civil Defense drills, while their parents built underground fallout shelters in the back yard.

Terror about the Stalinist red menace made FBI Director J. Edgar Hoover's wiretapping and the blacklisting of American citizens by Sen. Joseph McCarthy and the House Un-American Activities Committee seem acceptable. It all came to a halt when CBS's Edward R. Murrow and Fred Friendly courageously said, "Good night and good luck," to the junior senator from Wisconsin.

Today, our threat is mostly faceless with the exception of a recently deceased, unusually tall Arab on a dialysis machine. From perceived abuses of the Patriot Act to the debate over the legality of torture and humiliation as seen at Abu Ghraib prison and incarcerations at Guantanamo Bay, even the most stalwart of conservative legislators are asking if we have gone a little too far in the name of national security. It has taken John McCain, a Republican senator, who was himself a victim of torture as a POW in Vietnam, to say enough is enough.

The Whiz Kids

A brash young group of business intelligentsia was poised to rule the world in the '50s.

In his book, *The Best and The Brightest*, David Halberstam writes about these famed "Whiz Kids," a group of statistical savants from the Harvard Business School faculty that included Robert McNamara and Tom Rath. They had been recruited by the U.S. Army during World War II to develop a plan to build our armed forces.

Robert McNamara epitomized the Whiz Kids' "discipline, concentration and relentless work all day and night" ethic, Halberstam writes. "That work ethic grew the Army Air Corps from 295 pilots the year before Pearl Harbor to 96,000 the year after."

Following World War II, the Whiz Kids were marketed to corporations as a group, eventually finding their home at the Ford Motor Company. Salted among its executive ranks, the Whiz Kids transformed and retooled Ford to make it a powerhouse. In the process they would change the face of American business. McNamara became a nearly mythic figure, rising to Ford's top ranks before being recruited for public service.

Today, there are no pensions rewarded to "company men" like McNamara and Tom Rath. Our heroes are not corporate men, but entrepreneurs of all genders, shapes and colors. A Gallup study found that 50 percent of the adult population of the United States wanted to be entrepreneurs.

For the first time in the country's history, there are more millionaires in America 50 years of age and younger than 50 years and older. *Forbes* reports that by the late 1990s, 72 percent of the 400 richest Americans are first-generation millionaires. Today's Whiz Kids are Google guys Larry Page and Sergey Brin, Michael Dell, eBay's Meg Whitman, and Jeff Bezos of Amazon.com. Pittsburgh's new economy Whiz Kids include Glen Meakem of Freemarkets, Ron Bianchini of Spinnaker Networks, Sean McDonald of Automated Health Care, the late Ron Morris of J.D. Warren, Lou Wheeler of Rapidigm, and Eric Cooper's gang from Fore Systems.

Interstate and Cell Phones

In the '50s, the opiate of the people was television. According to author Stuart Kallen, in the age of Uncle Miltie and Liberace, the number of TV sets in American homes grew from 7,000 in 1946 to 50 million by 1960.

Today, people question which technology we are more addicted to: the cell phone, the Internet or the Internet-enabled cell phone. Now, 140 million Americans, or 59 percent, own a cell phone. And some even refer to their favorite personal digital assistant (PDA) as "Crackberry."

In the 1950s, the big project connecting people to each other and building commerce was the construction of the Interstate Highway system. The Federal-Aid Highway Act of 1956, President Dwight Eisenhower's great achievement, led to 40,000 miles of new highway. Pennsylvania added 1,500 miles of its own, led by the 313-mile Keystone Shortway, now known as I-80. Today, the great connectivity frontier supplanting Ike's interstates is "convergence," the combining of wireless transmission, content and hand-held computers. We'll no longer carry our laptops, cell phones, personal digital assistants and portable DVD players in a big black bag. They'll be clipped to our belts in a single device.

Peyton Place, Wisteria Lane

Commuters riding the train to work in 1956 probably kept the covers of a potboiler about a small New England town carefully hidden as they read. Written by Grace Metalious, it was a steamy saga called *Peyton Place,* which chronicled the life and loves of Allison MacKenzie, Selena Cross and Rodney Harrington. When it hit bookstores in September of '56, the novel became an immediate best seller. Branded "filth" by nearly every reviewer, *Peyton Place* would eventually sell more than 12 million copies. The television version starring Ryan O'Neal, Barbara Parkins and Mia Farrow made $62 million for its network.

Today, as we stand in line waiting for a skinny, double-shot grande to help us with our commute, we'd freely admit to knowing the décor of every house on Wisteria Lane, the home of our favorite *Desperate Housewives.* In comparison with the steam and relative earning power of *Peyton Place,* the exploits of Bree, Susan, Lynette and Edie are pretty tame. Compared with *Peyton Place's* "good parts," '50s code words for sex scenes, the murders and basement incarcerations of *Desperate Housewives* seem like an ABC-TV after-school special.

I Still Like Ike

On balance, things are surprisingly similar to 1950s' life. People want their slice of the American Dream. They want to fit in, and they want to get ahead. They enjoy new gadgets. They like a good yarn. They are afraid.

Perhaps the history professors weren't fooling. History does seem to repeat itself, though there are some stark differences between 1956 and 2006. Everything moves a little too fast now, we are under a lot of pressure and we sure like to over-extend ourselves financially.

So maybe it might not be a bad idea to call up Marty McFly and ask him to take us for a spin in his souped-up DeLorean.

THE HUSTLER OR *THE COLOR OF MONEY?*

After his death, I watched a lot of Paul Newman movies. His performances sometimes made me think about CEOs and how they seem to get better with age. That notion is particularly striking when I watch Newman play the character Eddie Felson in *The Hustler* and *The Color of Money.*

The young Felson in *The Hustler* just wants to be the "Fat Man," the legendary pool shark Minnesota Fats, played by Jackie Gleason. Then there is the sage Felson of Martin Scorsese's *The Color of Money*, who tries to impart the wisdom of years of experience to the headstrong Vincent Lauria, a gifted young player portrayed by Tom Cruise.

"You gotta have two things to win," Felson tells Vincent, after the young player has blown a hustle by showing off his skills. "You gotta have brains and you gotta have balls. Now, you got too much of one and not enough of the other." To work at finding this balance is good advice for most any entrepreneur.

Paul Newman won the Best Actor Academy Award for the the Felson role in *The Color of Money.* He didn't win it for his words, but for the silences, tilted head and attitude of a veteran.

Guru Stew

It's been six years since I left my post as CEO of a tech company after 16 years with the firm, nine of them at the helm. Since then, as a venture investor and board member of a couple of emerging companies, I've seen a lot of CEOs in action. I've looked at a lot of private investment deals, and I've done some CEO coaching as a teacher and public speaker. Most important, I've gotten a lot of distance from my CEO job. Now I see as many deficiencies in my performance as accomplishments.

For months, I've been trying to find just the right word to describe my evolution. It's pretty simple: age.

A couple of years before our tech company's stock price really took off, a local newspaper wrote a business profile about me. The article was titled "Guru Stew," because my management style was an amalgam of approaches culled from motivational experts ranging from Steven Covey to Anthony Robbins. It may have appeared that I was trying to be "leading edge," when, in fact, I was searching.

I tried everything from making my management team read a new book every week, to studying the Walt Disney Company's management practices, to modeling our product development process after the engineering methods and organizational skills of world-class auto racing teams.

Three months after the article appeared, we lost my Dad and our company's founder, Craig Allison, to a heart attack. In many ways, I lost someone who helped ground me. We had passionate discussions about management decisions. More often than not, we got to the same place, but by different routes.

Two years later, company revenues had doubled. Market capitalization hit $2 billion. Our tech company was lauded in the business sections of local newspapers. I was hailed as a management genius. Then Cinderella's clock struck midnight. Thousands of Americans died in an instant on September 11, 2001. The tech bubble burst.

After those events, I finally settled on the management approach that seemed best to me. I found it in a book called *The Practice of Management* by Peter Drucker, written in 1954. Drucker focuses on the classic philosophy of "management by objective," which centers on creating goals for each department in a company. The overarching organizational goal is finding customers and delivering better products that create better value for those customers. Sounds boring, yet it is sublime. Focused and boring are key to long-term success. Along with industry experience.

Here's the point. It took me years to get there. Was that a function of my being open-minded or simply not seeing enough? As I look back, I find myself not smiling about the good old days but thinking, "If only I knew then what I know now."

Age Trumps Enthusiasm

When talking about CEO performance, Dad used to say, "I'd rather throw water on a raging conflagration than try to light a damp pile of kindling." Dad believed enthusiasm trumps lack of experience.

But does it? I asked a prominent venture capitalist friend whether he bets on horses or jockeys. That is, when he makes an investment decision, is the company's business model more important, or is the experience of the management team?

"I invest in horses," my friend said. "I can always hire jockeys." In his opinion, it's harder to find the new, new thing than it is to find the right executives.

Far be it from me to question my friend's experienced and highly successful views, but it seems to me that it sure helps when you find a CEO with brains, poise and a little gray at the temples.

In all the deals I've evaluated over the last six years, I've focused on the CEO more than the business model. I've observed that a lot of the local economic development agencies seem to direct their attention to management as well. Once these emerging companies get the management thing figured out, the rest seems to take care of itself.

It's not that younger executives lack intellect or academic training. They just haven't seen as much. In my case, had I had more Zen than zest, my life as a CEO would've been a lot easier. But if I hadn't constantly been pushing myself and my troops, would we have done as well as we did? Would we have grown as fast and survived the speed bumps?

In his book *Moneyball*, Michael Lewis examines the groundbreaking approach of Billy Beane, general manager of the Oakland Athletics baseball team. Until Beane, most major league prospects were drafted right out of high school, based on scouts' expectations on how they would perform. Beane drafts players based on how they *have* performed. He drafts college players who have seen a lot of pitches.

Many people are promoted to CEO as a function of being the entrepreneurial founder of a company or a wunderkind at a big corporation; they may have seen only one or two business cycles. They've also probably seen only one or two major technological shifts, and in many cases, the current economy is the only major financial downturn they've ever experienced.

Reports I've read say that in 2007 the median age of S&P 500 CEOs was 55. Another indicated that less than a third of the 2,258 S&P 500 CEOs who left their jobs between 1995 and 2007 were hired before the age of 47. Just like Billy Beane's players, these executives had seen a lot of pitches. So most of the people hired as CEOs are about the age I am now.

A third study said "the average and median age of key tech founders was 39." I was 34 years old when I became CEO of a tech company and 44 when I left.

I would relish the chance to jump into the time tunnel and return to 1988, when we started the company, and be armed with not only the perspective I've gained, but also the intellectual insights I've developed as a college professor studying management practices.

There might be a problem, though.

I like having more time to spend with my wife. I'm much more risk-averse than I was then. I like being able to get a good night's sleep. And I like eating properly and exercising every day.

Most of all, I like not needing what I used to call "The High Tech Fun Pack," which consisted of a popular sleep aid, a tablet for heartburn and a capsule for gastrointestinal distress.

But it's an interesting thought, isn't it?

DREAMS AND BANKERS

A local restaurant owner we'll call "Sam" dreamed of revitalizing his sleepy little borough near a major metropolitan area. He wanted to improve not only the business at his four-star restaurant, but also the financial health of the merchants around him.

Sam's dream slowly became a crucible, as the forces of easy money and lax lending practices converged to defeat him just when he thought he was going to win. His plight illustrates the fate of many businesses born of the go-go '90s, when too many Americans didn't realize that if it sounds too good to be true, it usually is.

Typically decked out in jeans, black T-shirt, artsy thick-soled shoes and facial stubble, Sam is a chef, economic developer and music aficionado. He also is a classic lifestyle entrepreneur.

Lifestyle entrepreneurs tend to run businesses that provide a good standard of living. Their businesses are not run by following detailed cash-flow plans or high-level management practices. The businesses are started with a small amount of capital—most with as little as $25,000. Many are retail operations. And these small businesses really drive our economy, because they employ more than half the people in the United States.

In many ways Sam epitomizes the successful lifestyle entrepreneur. Shoot from the hip and be hip when you shoot. Have great product, unique service, customer intimacy and love. Keep all the numbers in your head, not on some Excel spreadsheet that nobody will read.

Lifestyle entrepreneurs know their customers because they speak to them every night. They know them so well that demographic statistics and econometric trend reports don't mean squat. What carries weight is the primary research these entrepreneurs conduct with their customers every day. And just as squirrels know to hide nuts in the fall, lifestyle entrepreneurs have a sixth business sense, usually learned in the school of hard knocks.

Conversely, "high-growth" entrepreneurs develop detailed business plans and raise significant capital from professional investors to create large businesses and rapid revenue growth. Managers have a high level of experience in the industry's target market. The objective is selling the business through a merger or an initial public offering that gives investors a superior return.

Test Case: The Small Township

After leaving a good gig running a major corporation's cafeteria, Sam and his wife, Lori, opened his restaurant in 1999. People were flush with cash and the Pittsburgh fine-dining scene was beginning to blossom. Sam was head chef and Lori ran the front of the house, also serving as pastry chef.

Sam didn't buy into the real estate mantra of location, location, location. He chose the borough, eschewing higher-rent locations, a downtown metropolitan city location or upscale suburbs, where "foodies" live and work. He took the *Field of Dreams* approach, "build it and they will come." All he'd need was great food.

Foodies' lives revolve around the Food Network and dining "experiences;" they loved Sam's simple approach of grilling whatever expensive and exotic raw ingredients came to mind. Business boomed. Customers had to call two weeks ahead for a table. Awards from local magazines and positive reviews multiplied. After risking so much, Sam and Lori felt life was finally coming together.

Then, some terrorists decided to fly planes into the World Trade Center and high-flying dot.coms crashed on Wall Street, too. Sam saw his restaurant's business slow, as diners, eyeing much skinnier 401k plans, reduced their midweek meals out. Sam couldn't fall back on locals, typical small town residents, because they reserved fine dining only for special occasions. To make matters worse, competition was cropping up.

Sam decided to combat the malaise by making his borough—not just his restaurant—a destination. Unlike typical restaurant goers, foodies will leave the beaten path for a new experience, going from one trendy new spot to the next. Attracting them was critical for Sam's business. So he dreamed big. He'd create a local Greenwich Village, with cool coffee shops, offbeat fast food and funky retail.

If I build it, they will come. Shoot from the hip and be hip when you shoot. And my businesses will benefit.

Sam became a one-man gang of economic development. He encouraged his sister and brother-in-law to create an edgy hot dog shop, helping them develop the concept and menu. The shop's sausages, homemade soups and sides were featured in local print outlets and on TV. Business was good.

Sam's next project was to create a coffee shop with attitude. The finest coffees, teas, fresh baked goods and panini sandwiches were served in a combination coffee shop and art gallery. The clientele was young and artsy.

He encouraged an Italian pizza maker to create a Neapolitan bistro, which also did well.

Sam's big vision for the borough was starting to come together. But the small town needed some sort of "anchor" store. His *pièce de résistance* would be the creation of a high-end department store for vintage clothing in a renovated G.C. Murphy building that had been standing vacant for a few years.

After recruiting a handful of investors, Sam obtained a high-interest subprime mortgage to buy the empty building. And just as he had done in his restaurants, Sam and his merry band of local free spirits would complete all the construction on a shoestring with used and lower-cost building materials from boutique building product stores.

The anchor store would be called "517/521," its address in the borough. Downstairs it would be a cross between a consignment shop and a vintage department store, where a variety of independent storeowners would operate their own "departments." Each department would rent space, and the store would get a percentage of sales for managing operations, including building maintenance and paying cashiers. Upstairs would be a multipurpose working space for artists and writers.

Sam had his subprime loan and a little investment money, along with financing collateralized by his other properties. He had his anchor building. The process had been quite easy. Maybe too easy.

Where's Mr. Banks?

When our financial system nearly froze in 2007, many of us started to wonder how the conservative Mr. Banks from *Mary Poppins* became pull-out-the-stops Gordon Gekko from *Wall Street*. What happened to the conservative lending standards that made us feel our money was safe? When did our mortgage lender turn from community partner to someone selling an addictive elixir in the shadows?

In years past, small business owners underwent exhaustive application procedures to obtain financing. A loan officer evaluated the loan application and, most importantly, the business itself. Due diligence. Face-to-face meetings with the applicant and the applicant's customers. How did business look for the near term? The long term? What was the applicant's track record on other borrowing? Could the business generate enough money to pay back the loan?

If the application looked good, the loan officer developed a detailed loan request or "write up," which was submitted to the bank's loan committee. If, after discussion, the loan committee approved the loan, the loan officer held regular follow-up meetings with the business owner. The owner was also charged with advising the lender if his business began having problems. If the situation got really bad, the loan would go into "work out," which many times resulted in a restructuring or, in the worst case, liquidation.

Too Good To Be True

With Sam, none of this took place. He got his loan with minimal interaction with the mortgage company. No site visits or regular follow-ups. No ongoing relationship between lender and borrower.

Sam had secured enough money to buy the building and open it, but he didn't have enough capital to see the store filled with inventory. Rental of department spaces was creating decent income, but sales in the departments were not brisk. Without sufficient percentage of sales income, it was difficult for Sam to find the cash to complete build-outs for new tenants. Cash flow became even more strained when some of his larger tenants were late paying rent due to bureaucratic foul-ups. Sam was forced to subsidize the building's operation when rent couldn't cover the high monthly cost of the subprime mortgage.

After failing to sell the building and restructuring the debt with the lender, Sam threw in the towel. He handed the keys to the mortgage company, which was painful to his credit rating and his state of mind. The word "quit" is anathema to an entrepreneur like Sam.

So he pulled up stakes and moved to a town with a much higher per capita income. Now, his restaurant is thriving.

Yes, Sam would have benefited from a bank that was a partner, not a pusher. A thorough loan officer might have helped him foresee and avoid problems from the beginning. Maybe more capital for contingencies. Maybe a better business plan. But Sam, classic lifestyle entrepreneur, probably wouldn't have liked those ideas. Shoot from the hip and be hip when you shoot. If I build it, they will come.

Come they did. Just not fast enough to pay the mortgage.

DR. JEKYLL AND MR. ENTREPRENEUR

Oscar Levant, pianist, composer, actor and native Pittsburgher, once quipped: "There's a fine line between genius and insanity. I have erased this line."

You don't need to spend a lot of time with entrepreneurs to realize that while the line between genius and insanity for them may not be erased, it is certainly smudged. For each Willie Loman, a Willy Wonka. A Dr. Jekyll for every Mr. Hyde.

You see in entrepreneurs huge capacity for risk. You discern obsessiveness. You recognize quick, restless minds. You notice a constant need to prove their worth—to others and, more importantly, to themselves. They must control.

While they may start their businesses out of intellectual curiosity, lingering in the back of their minds is a desire to forever end having to click their heels in front of a dullard's desk. They want to accumulate "screw you" wealth.

Their biggest fear is not failure. It is boredom. They curse the darkness of the status quo and self-immolate to illuminate change.

Hypomania

Perhaps great entrepreneurs aren't technically crazy, but they sure aren't like most people.

Author Michael Lewis calls the entrepreneur a frontiersman and describes him this way: "Really, there is no good word for what he does. I first noticed this problem when I watched one of those people—a man who had made himself a billion dollars—try to fill in a simple questionnaire. On the line that asked him to state his occupation, he did not know what to write. Searcher? He couldn't very well put that down."

Psychologist John D. Gartner takes it a step further in his book, *The Hypomaniac Edge: The Link Between (A Little) Craziness and (A Lot) of Success in America.* He describes hypomania as "an elevated mood state that feels 'highly intoxicating, powerful, productive and desirable' to the hypomaniac." This mood state, Gartner argues, helps us understand historical figures like Christopher Columbus, Alexander Hamilton, John Winthrop, William Penn and Andrew Carnegie. It also helps us understand today's entrepreneurs.

My Dad

Take my late father, R. Craig Allison, for example. He started many companies in his lifetime. He started a plastics company, a safety barricade business, a concrete contracting company, a street repair and gas pipeline company, a consumer electronics repair business, a cable-television provider and a maker of telecommunications test equipment.

Some of these start-ups were failures, some moderate successes, and the last emerged as a Wall Street-traded public company. Sadly, my Dad didn't live to see that home run sail out of the park and bounce into the Allegheny.

Yet with all of this chutzpah and success, he never felt himself worthy. My Dad wanted to prove to others that he could belong to the best clubs, have the best house, and be "a player" in the financial big leagues. Success was a way to get back at those he felt looked down on him throughout his life. His entrepreneurship was his self-justification, his vengeance.

He had a rapid-fire mind and could grasp abstracts quickly. A lifelong insomniac, he would regularly call me at 2 a.m. to tell me to turn on the television and see the germ of his latest brainstorm. He had what people call "vision." When he tried starting a cable company, the industry was in its infancy. He predicted the growth of cell phones in the early '80s. He foresaw that DSL would revolutionize communication in the '90s.

My Dad understood how to raise capital and what motivated people to invest. The $6 million in start-up money he raised to create his tech company in the late '80s and early '90s became a business valued at $72.6 million on the day of its IPO on December 14, 1995. By 2000, the company had reached a market capitalization of $2 billion.

A fiercely loyal family man, his anonymous philanthropy was generous and far-reaching.

But there was a sad, dark side to my Dad. His mental highs touched the stratosphere and his lows were deeper than the Mariana Trench. While he could be rib-crampingly funny, his temper was legendary.

He battled his weight all his life, knowing it could eventually kill him. He had a heart bypass in 1978 at the ripe old age of 37 and a second procedure in 1992. He endured more than 20 cardiac angiograms and multiple angioplasties and stents through the years.

My Dad was 5'8" tall and weighed more than 200 pounds. He was diabetic, which, for a person with heart disease, is like having someone throw gasoline on your backyard barbecue. Still, he didn't watch what he ate. And after his death in 1998 at age 57, my mother found a pack of cigarettes in his pocket.

R. Craig Allison had enormous capacity for risk powered by eternal optimism. His last day on earth, he was working on the details of a bio-tech start-up and a metals processing start-up.

Entrepreneurs like my Dad have unique personalities that lift up the economy and make life better for the rest of us more conventional folks. They deserve our thanks and our prayers that, along with the gold they found at the end of the rainbow, they also found peace.

RON MORRIS,
AN ENTREPRENEUR'S
ENTREPRENEUR

Ever been stranded in the automotive purgatory of a highway construction zone? Did you find yourself secretly admiring the driver who flies down the passing lane and darts into the merge point at the last possible moment? Well, your traffic jam hero was probably an entrepreneur.

This breed tends to ask for forgiveness rather than seek permission. They have no problem using the other sex's restroom if the appropriate lavatory is otherwise occupied. Hey, problem solved, right?

Entrepreneurs think outside the box and have an incredible tolerance for risk. In his seminal textbook, *The Entrepreneur's Guide to Finance and Business*, Steven Rogers points out that the average entrepreneur fails 3.8 times before succeeding. Look up the definition of "undaunted" in an illustrated dictionary and you'll find a picture of an entrepreneur.

They tend to interrupt you when you're talking, ask a lot of questions and have unquiet minds. When facing a monumental decision, an entrepreneur's typical question is, "What's the worst that can happen?"

Most importantly, entrepreneurs create most of the jobs in this country. According to a study by economists John Haltiwanger of the University of Maryland and Ron Jarmin and Javier Miranda of the U.S. Census Bureau, from

1992 to 2005 all net job increases in the United States were created by start-up businesses, not large, mature corporations.

Wants to be a millionaire? Yep, that's an entrepreneur. But entrepreneurs prefer that the money be the result of their ability and effort. Data in Thomas J. Stanley's best-selling *The Millionaire Mind* shows that most millionaires in the United States don't inherit wealth. They want their compensation tied to performance, not longevity.

When I hear the word entrepreneur, I always think of my friend, Ron Morris.

In addition to starting without external capital more than seven successful businesses, mostly in the technology space, and creating significant wealth for himself in the process, Ron was one of the biggest advocates for entrepreneurism in our region.

He founded and for the last decade has led the Entrepreneurial Studies Program at Duquesne University, which has educated hundreds of students in the sometimes Faustian art of starting businesses. I've heard Ron emphasize that being one's own boss does not come without a reasonable level of strife and personal sacrifice.

His nationally syndicated radio broadcast, *The American Entrepreneur*, inspired thousands to start their own businesses. A regular columnist for the Pittsburgh Technology Council's *TEQ* magazine, he wrote prolifically about how to create successful new ventures.

Finally, and possibly most importantly, Ron provided start-up capital and board advice to dozens of local businesses as an active angel investor.

These feats are not those of a mere mortal. Six years ago, Ron began a battle against serious cancer. He lost his fight in the summer of 2012.

Heroic? A genius? Inspiring? He'd scoff if I described him in those terms. Let's leave it at this. Ron Morris was an entrepreneur's entrepreneur.

SAY WHAT?
THE CRAZY LANGUAGE OF
START-UP CAPITAL

If you think it's hard understanding a George Will column, you ought to spend time with the technology intelligentsia as they evaluate a prospective investment in a start-up company.

Every industry has its own vernacular, but this gang can befuddle the most erudite among us.

Show Me the Money: Names for Start-Up Investors

In the world of high-risk investment, people who buy stock in private start-up companies have names ranging from "friends and family" to "angels" and "venture capitalists."

"Friends and family" means just what you think. However, the start-up reference manuals at Barnes & Noble neglect to tell you the risks if you blow their money. If you do, you probably won't be able to sit at the cool kids' table on Thanksgiving Day.

After you've exhausted Mom and Dad's vacation money, you'll climb the investment food chain to "angels." High-tech angel investors often are rich people with way too much time on their hands. According to an article published by the Harvard Business School, "the term 'angel' originated in the early 1900s and referred to investors on Broadway who made risky investments to support theatrical productions." Today's angel investors "pony up" for two reasons. First, they want to generate better returns than the S&P 500. Second, they like the action.

Most angels are successful entrepreneurs. Entrepreneurs start companies for personal freedom and the thrill of the game. After they make their pile of dough through a buy-out or some other "liquidity event," they go through a business jones that can only be satisfied by dabbling in another start-up company between rounds of golf and attending charity events.

"Guardian angels" also give start-up companies economical "been there, done that" management help. This assistance is invaluable, because fledgling companies cannot afford executives or management consultants with such a high level of expertise and experience.

An ironic saying among start-up CEOs is, "It's easier to raise $5 million than $500,000." That's because venture capitalists, a main source of speculative funding, must invest at least $1 million in a company. It's a matter of portfolio management.

A good venture capital firm will hit big on two out of the 10 investments in its "portfolio." According to Steven Rogers in *The Entrepreneur's Guide to Finance and Business*, seven percent of a venture firm's investments account for the majority of its profits. Another reason for the $1 million threshold is "bandwidth." Venture capital firms aren't that big in terms of headcount. It takes as much time for a VC to evaluate and keep tabs on a $500,000 investment as it does a $5 million investment. There are only so many deals in the day.

Venture capitalists are fascinated with something called "burn rate." A start-up's "burn" is the cash it consumes every 30 days because the company isn't selling enough products with gross profits sufficient to cover expenses. In a lot of cases, entrepreneurs really don't know how much cash their businesses will need to reach profitability because they have underestimated the monthly burn rate.

VCs are experts at these and other calculations, leading some people to refer to them as "vulture capitalists." I hate that term because often it's the wine of sour grapes, uttered by start-up company founders who should have spent more time developing and realistically scrutinizing their business plan.

When it comes to business valuations, "comparable market prices" rule. A "comp" is a company with similar characteristics to yours in the same industry. If somebody paid x to invest in a company similar to yours, more than likely you're not going to get x + 1 for your company, not unless you have one hell of a beautiful new idea.

And beauty is always in the eye of the beholder. This is where you'll learn about "the golden rule." No, not that one. In the venture capital world, it's "Whoever has the gold, rules."

Another name for venture capital is "private equity." The difference between private and public equity is simple. Private equity firms make investments for clients by buying stock in companies not traded on a public market exchange, such as the New York Stock Exchange or NASDAQ. Public equity firms are called stock brokers.

Making the Pitch

The process of raising private equity for your start-up is called "the deal."

Imagine yourself entering the office of a well-heeled venture capital firm to seek investment in your whiz-bang new idea: a dental floss dispenser for IPODs.

You walk into a technology-laden conference room that resembles the command center on the cable series *24*. The walls are covered with framed "tombstones." Tombstones are announcements of successful financial transactions printed on little vellum cards and mailed to prospective and existing clients of investment companies. An ominous way of announcing something good has happened, right?

You'll be greeted by the smiling face of one of the firm's partners. Don't be intimidated, even though it's likely the partner attended Stanford, Carnegie Mellon or Harvard Business School, after having spent five years as a nuclear engineer or molecular biologist. Also in the room are some of the partner's clients, a small group of potential investors.

In the world of start-up money, your "pitch" is a 20-minute oral presentation about your business idea accompanied by 15 fancy, well-animated PowerPoint slides. During your pitch, you should present a customer problem that is solved by your proprietary product in a huge, addressable market that has yet to be penetrated. Having a patented product is a nice touch.

A few minutes into the pitch, you'll figure out which investors like what they're hearing, because you'll start hearing some fun new words from them.

One prospective investor might inquire if your business is in a "vertical" or "horizontal" market. You might be stumped, believing it was sufficient for the market to be big, and not important that it was upright or reclining. The distinction is important, however. A "vertical" market is one where you sell the same customers a lot of different stuff. A "horizontal" market is where you sell a lot of different customers the same stuff.

Another investor may ask how you will protect your "FMA." FMA stands for "First Mover Advantage." First Mover Advantage is not leaving the Pirates game at the bottom of the eighth inning to beat the traffic. It's selling a bunch of your stuff before anybody gets the bright idea to copy your idea because there is a lot of money to be made selling stuff like yours, but less expensively.

Another investor will ask you about your "IP." You might be inclined to respond, "No. I stopped by the gas station before I got here." Don't do that. IP is investor-speak for "intellectual property." If you haven't already spent a lot of money with an attorney who specializes in filing patents, the investor may take you to task on the matter. What's the difference between patent applied for, patent pending and patent held? About $25,000 in legal fees.

Almost There

Providing that your pitch and discussion have gone well, you'll begin to discuss "valuation," that is, how much your company is worth. For investors that means how much of your start-up company they will get in exchange for the cash they invest.

During this chat, you'll hear more new terms. The investors will want to review your "pre-money" valuation and "post-money" valuation. "Pre-money" is not copper, silver and gold before they get melted and molded into coins. It is the value of your company before these venture capitalists invest. "Post-money" is not how they mail you the check. It is the value of the company after you get the money.

Since they're in the business of making big sums of money, the potential investors in your aforementioned dental floss dispenser for IPADs gizmo will start suggesting ways the "pre-money" valuation of your company must be discounted. You and your management team are inexperienced; that's a discount. Your product isn't manufactured and on the market yet; that's a discount. There's a discount if your company doesn't have a big-name customer. There's a discount if your company isn't profitable. There's a discount if you watch *Dancing with the Stars* and vote for your favorite couple regularly, and so on.

Finally, the prospective investors will want to discuss your thoughts about an "exit strategy." Responding that you were planning to take the Parkway if you got out of the meeting before 5 p.m. is not a good answer. In start-up investing terminology, "exit strategy" is how the investors will get their money back, along with a return of, say, five to 10 times their original investment.

Toward the end of the meeting, they'll mention that a condition of their investment will be three seats on the board of directors of your start-up firm; a seat for one of the investors, a seat for an industry expert they've known for years and a seat for the former CEO of a company in which they've previously invested. They'll leave two seats for your company's management. No, there's nothing wrong with your math. Three for them and two for you means that they can whack you if you screw up.

That's "the deal."

Now, you may feel like excusing yourself, informing your prospective investors that while you are grateful for their time and interest, your request for this meeting was a bad idea. You are instead going to attempt an assault on K-2 in Nepal, since your climb of that mountain seems to have a much more reasonable prospect for success.

Or, you might stand, shake each individual's hand, and ask when you can expect to receive the documents for signature.

IMAGE AND REALITY

Aboard an international flight bound for Ireland from Philadelphia, I was reminded of the Texas saying, "He's all hat and no cattle."

I'd just buckled into my seat next to my wife Jane, experiencing the Zen-like relief of having made our international connection by the skin of our teeth. We were sweating profusely.

From the seat back in front of me I pulled out the in-flight magazine and began to read "Our New Team," a letter from the airline's CEO. "We know how important it is to our customers to get to their destination on time without having their travel plans disrupted," the CEO assured me.

Now that particular day, I could have introduced the CEO to at least 17 people who had missed their international connections and probably would have accused him of selling snake oil in his stupid letter, right before they went all Floyd Mayweather on him.

That's what got me thinking about cows and big Stetson hats. What most frustrated my fellow travelers was the fact that the four-hour delay we'd experienced getting to Philadelphia was not a result of weather or a mechanical problem. We had a waiting plane but no crew.

Our crew had been delayed in Hartford. When their aircraft finally touched down, most of my fellow international travelers still had a shot at making their flights. But, sticking to the letter of the work rules in an acrimoniously negotiated contract, our crew stopped to eat lunch on the way to our gate.

Granted, they were entitled to take the break, but according to the airline crew people I chatted with, the pilots and flight attendants were so angry about the new contract that they no longer skipped breaks as they might have done in the past in the interests of getting people somewhere on time.

When the gate agents heard about this gastronomical insult to injury, they quietly snuck away for their shift change to avoid the wrath of passengers. I can't say I blamed them. I wouldn't relish telling a family of seven they were going to miss their cruise ship in Italy because some guy needed a hoagie real bad.

I continued reading the CEO's letter. "The sole focus of the agents who staff the centers," he wrote, "will be getting customers who have missed their flights, due to delays or cancellations, onto another flight to their destination as soon as possible."

When we did finally arrive in Philadelphia, there was no agent at the gate to direct us to the international gates. As he was deplaning, an off-duty crew person who'd caught a hop on our flight told us, "Yeah, those folks kind of disappear on the weekend." Fortunately, he was able to point us toward the international gates, which were a Bataan death march away from our arrival concourse.

Had it not been for the friendly airport golf-cart driver who gave us a lift, we would never have made the flight. We would have had to cut short our vacation while incurring the expense of a hotel room in Philadelphia. The driver pulled up to our gate just as the doors of the plane were closing. As we scurried off, we gave our airport Samaritan a $20 tip. He was so grateful, you'd have thought we'd offered to pay his kid's college tuition. Given that he'd saved our vacation, it was the least we could do.

Our adventure had occurred despite the CEO's solemn promise in his letter. "The best part about this new resource for customers is that they will be met at the gate by a member of the team," he wrote.

All hat and no cattle. Quite simply, the CEO's letter was a masterpiece of public relations written by a gang of marketers without any basic grasp of reality. I envisioned a cabal of Marshall McLuhan wannabes on the airline's public relations team mapping out the post-merger publicity campaign.

In a conference room at the airline's headquarters, some team leader wearing Gucci loafers and no socks wrote bullet point No. 1: "CEO letter for airline magazine." Bullet point No. 2 was probably: "Highlight investment in ticket agents and ground staff, a new Passenger Control Center and better personal communication."

Sound like great ideas. If only they were true.

Unfortunately, our airline had made strategic decisions that led to delayed flights and angry customers, all in the interest of justifying to Wall Street that its merger with another airline would create a more profitable company. Redesignating hubs, introducing regional jets and ruthlessly renegotiating union contracts led to clogged traffic and low worker morale. Of course, you can't see those results from a PR flack's office, or from the CEO's, for that matter.

The airline's advertising and public relations folks are forging the image of a carrier with on-time flights and great customer service. Yet reality belies the image. The number of flight delays is egregious and too often there is an utter lack of communication between agents and passengers.

That doesn't bode well for long-term profitability, no matter the short-term gains Wall Street may have taken.

If the airline really wanted its image to match its identity, I can help. The new slogan would be simple.

"You're stuck."

THE WALK OF TRUTH

Mark Twain referred to golf as "a good walk spoiled," but I like to think of golf as a journey of revelation. A round can reveal whether you really want to do business with someone. "If there is any larceny in a man," an unknown golfer once said, "a golf game will bring it out."

On a basic level, executives golf with customers and business associates because it gives them four hours of uninterrupted time together, a rarity in our frenetic world of smart phones, GPS systems and constant access. In those four hours, some basic elements of human nature surface: how disposed you are to lie, cheat or steal; how you approach life in general; how courageous and determined you are; and, finally, how likely you are to take yourself too seriously.

I undertook the game when I was well into my 40s, which some say is a huge mistake. Although I practice a lot, I'm not very good. But I am observant, and I like watching people as they play. Mostly, they make me laugh. Not because of their lack of proficiency (living in a glass house somewhere way over par, I never throw stones). No, I find humor in their constant efforts to fool others and themselves.

The Ability To Count, Literally

First and most basically, golf will help you decide if you can jump into bed with someone on a business deal and not get more than a good night's sleep. Just observe how a potential associate scores his game.

We've all played with golfers who are arithmetically challenged. Some of these players may also be "long" or "large" off the tee; they can hit the crap out of it. But a tee shot approaching 300 yards sometimes can be errant as well. So errant, in fact, that it bounces its way out of bounds (OB).

If a golfer suspects he's OB, it's sometimes wise for him to take another, provisional, tee shot just in case the ball from the first tee shot can't be found. In that event, the second tee shot is scored as a third shot. You count the first shot off the tee and a penalty stroke for being OB. So your second tee shot is actually your third shot. This is called "hitting three."

When someone scores a hole and "forgets" he was hitting three, you should ask yourself: If he's less than forthright about something as trivial as a golf score, how honest will he be filling out an expense report or honoring a verbal contract? As golfing great Jimmy Demaret said, "Golf is based on honesty. Where else would you admit to a seven on a par three?"

Taking Your Turn

In golf, playing properly is more critical than playing well.

I've always imagined that the person who developed golf etiquette must've read the New Testament. General conduct falls under the Book of Luke. "Do unto others as you would have them do unto you."

On the course you should avoid making noise or moving around when someone is preparing to swing the club or attempt a putt. That includes texting. Oh yeah, and make sure your cell phone is turned off.

Next is the Book of Matthew. "So the last shall be first," the gospel states, "and the first last: for many be called, but few chosen."

The golf translation would be, "Hey, dummy, I don't care how important you think you are or if you really, really want to finish that one out, it's my turn."

After someone hits a tee shot, or a second shot or is putting on the green, the person farthest away from the hole shoots first. And the person who wins a hole tees off first on the following hole. That is called "having honors."

It's all a real estate issue. When it's your turn, the line from your ball to the hole is your real estate, albeit only for a moment. And if someone disrespects your "property rights" on the golf course, how careful will he be developing a business plan? How assiduous when reviewing a balance sheet?

Focus, Temper and Adversity

Bobby Jones, the golfer of all golfers and probably the game's greatest gentleman, famously spoke about a person's ability to focus: "Golf is a game that is played on a five-inch course—the distance between your ears."

You can discern a colleague's ability to persevere when he soldiers on despite a bad start to a round. I'm always impressed by someone who shakes off a bad shot and hits a great follow-up. And I'm even more impressed if he can laugh at himself and not spoil our "good walk."

Of course, a bad temper on a golf course can be funny. Take the case of Craig "The Walrus" Stadler. "Why am I using a new putter?" he once said. "Because the old one didn't float too well." You can see poise or its absence pretty quickly on a golf course.

Will your golf partner drag the ball out of high rough to make the shot easier—*a la* Enron and off-balance-sheet partnerships? Or will he play with grace and aplomb the lie where he finds himself—*a la* Johnson & Johnson and the 1982 Tylenol scare?

During his career Bobby Jones began to suffer from a debilitating illness called syringomyelia, a spinal disease that withered him over the years. He was confined to a wheelchair and weighed less than 90 pounds when he died in 1971. "I will tell you privately," he confided to a friend as he declined, "it's not going to get better, it's going to get worse all the time, but don't fret. Remember, we 'play the ball where it lies,' and now let's not talk about this, ever again."

Now there's a golfer it would be an honor to do business with. And I know another.

A recent devotee of the game, my old boss Frankie at the public relations firm where I worked in the '80s was recently diagnosed with Parkinson's disease.

Frankie was a rabid physical-fitness junkie during those years. He earned a black belt in karate. He inspired me to get into physical fitness and stay with it. We worked out together almost every day that I was with the firm.

Frankie's doctors believe his devotion to exercise probably beat back the Parkinson's for much longer than is normal. It also may have made the disease undetectable for many years.

Since his diagnosis, Frankie hasn't been able to work out as aggressively as he once did. But he's taken up golf. In just a year, he's developed an impressive game.

One day I invited him to play a round at my country club. As we approached the first hole, he pulled out a copious set of notes on each hole. He'd gone to the club's web site, studied the course and planned out exactly how he would play each hole, right down to yardage, position and club selection.

I had to grin to myself. Remember what I said about revelation? Here was the same guy I remembered from 30 years ago, recording in precise detail each and every one of our workouts at the gym.

Frankie is good-humored about a bad shot. He recovers quickly. And he records every stroke, because he is adamant about improving his score.

My friend is using his golf game to slow a terrible disease. He's finding hope.

Frankie may not be as physical as he once was, but he remains active and in good spirits. He's "playing the ball where it lies."

I'd do business with a guy like that in a heartbeat.

BIG DADDY

A few years ago, I traveled down South to attend the funeral of the top salesperson our tech company had during my tenure as CEO. Then and ever since, I've thought a lot about what makes a great salesperson.

Wayne had many customers. I watched them file by the dozen past his casket. Some had loaded their wife and kids in the car and driven 15 hours to get there. Seeing them pay their respects helped me understand how Wayne made his quotas for us, month in and month out, for more than 12 years.

My late father, the founder of our company, liked to say, "Nothing happens until a sale is made." Wayne, like my father, looked at solving problems for customers as if he was solving problems for his own family. Whether the problem was related to work or home, Wayne was everyone's father. That's why my nickname for him was "Big Daddy."

Big Daddy was a barrel-chested bear of a man with the guile of a fox and the heart of a lion. He loved having his family living with him in his hard-earned sprawling home on a quiet lake in Alabama. The only problem was that he spent little time there. Our company's Southern road warrior left home early Monday morning and didn't return until Friday night.

Well into his 60s, Big Daddy was "country strong." I can still picture this burly man carrying two mammoth hard-shell suitcases through Atlanta's

Hartsfield Airport along with a briefcase full of computers and cell phones, like some giant hermit crab skittering along the Information Superhighway.

Big Daddy always packed a full week's worth of clothes in the suitcases, so he could stay with his customers, no matter how long it took to solve a problem.

But he certainly wasn't a clothes horse. Quite the contrary, he dressed in khaki pants; short-sleeve, button-down shirts and vibram-soled dress shoes. He wanted to be dressed the same way his telephone company engineer customers were. He knew it was important to fit in.

When people ran into Big Daddy at a company office, they thought that he was just another one of the "telephone men" who worked there. Not only did he look the part, he was as intellectually proficient as any Ma Bell techie.

Big Daddy was master of the low-pressure, soft-sell technique. When he visited customers, he wasn't there to sell the technical capabilities of our company's products. He was there to "ease their pain." He didn't sell telephone trouble-shooting systems, our company's stock in trade; he sold "makin' more of your customers happy."

Now Big Daddy could be pretty long-winded, holding onto a point like "a hound dog on a soup bone," but when I was with him on sales calls, I saw him *listen*. Big Daddy sold with his ear, not his mouth. He listened until he had figured out what the customer needed; he didn't simply peddle what he had in his samples case.

Big Daddy told me that the real selling was done during cigarette breaks, not during fancy PowerPoint presentations to big groups of "key decision makers." He believed that people didn't want to say what they were really thinking in front of groups for fear of saying the wrong thing in a highly political environment. Gaining customers' confidence was a private matter, the way he saw it.

There were tears in the eyes of Big Daddy's customers as they stood in front of his casket, and I realized that I was witnessing the true reason for his success. He was genuinely a friend. At the service, I listened to story upon story of Big Daddy attending the Little League games of his customers' children or sitting with a customer in a hospital waiting room when a loved one was facing a health crisis.

Big Daddy won his customers' trust by being a good man and a true friend. He figured out what his customers needed and provided it, even if it meant he would have to do battle with the company that wrote his commission checks. And that's what great selling is all about.

Godspeed, Big Daddy.

CONFESSIONS OF
A JOB JUNKIE

Two years after I left my job as CEO of a tech company, I felt I had just about made it through detox. But like every adrenalin addict—mine was the rush of running a start-up company that went public—I still felt pangs of regret.

Now, six years on, I still do. I miss the old gang at work. Sometimes I even miss the industry that had come both to terrify and bore me to tears.

As I was coming to terms with leaving my job, a friend reminded me that my departure was probably good for all concerned. "You know," he said, "sometimes they just get tired of looking at your face."

According to a *USA Today* article, "The average CEO tenure has shrunk to about five years, down from a long-term average of a decade." Since I sat in the boss's chair for nearly 10 years, I'd been using longer than most addicts.

Which is funny, since I got the CEO job because nobody else wanted it. Hell, I didn't want it, either.

I'll never forget getting a phone call from my late father, the company's founder, back in the early '90s.

"Look," he said, "I've got to pay attention to my other businesses, so you're running the company."

I hung up the phone and wondered what to do next. My job then was as a flack at a public relations agency. I wrote brochures. I didn't know the first thing about running a company, let alone a struggling start-up backed by a nervous group of angel investors from my hometown.

I sat wide awake at 3 a.m. in my apartment, like some loser in a Paul Simon album, watching TV. Then on came a Tony Robbins infomercial. I bit. With my *Personal Power* tapes playing in my earpieces, I started jogging every night in Shadyside.

From that beginning I learned a lot. I learned how to go back to irritated shareholders for more money when the company was strapped for cash. I learned how to sell telephone line-testing equipment to a highly technical group of customers. I learned how to take a company public and not choke on my toothbrush every quarter, wondering if we would make Wall Street analysts' estimates.

I began to live my life in 90-day increments. The name of the game was pleasing the analysts by growing the company. Please the analysts, you please the market. Please the market, you please the shareholders. We grew the company from nothing to more than $100 million in annual sales. In the year 2000, our tech company was valued at more than $2 billion. That's "billion" with a "b."

My face was plastered over the financial pages of newspapers and printed in the glossy, glowing feature articles of business magazines. It was quite a rush.

Then the telecom boom went bust. The irrational exuberance of the markets was replaced by the bunker mentality of only the strong survive. Osama bin Laden's minions flew airliners into the World Trade Center and the Pentagon. And life was never the same.

Like sailors on liberty, telecom companies had spent gobs of money investing in broadband service for the Internet revolution. Now they were left with an overbuilt network and warehouses stockpiled with gear that was collecting dust.

Technology was changing at a frantic pace, and our company was racing to keep up. Our bread-and-butter equipment was designed to test the old wired network. But the wired network was being replaced by a "virtual" network of Internet phone service delivery. And it was happening faster than anyone expected.

Big problem. It took 18 months to design and test a new product. It took another 18 months to weave through the maze of planning meetings, lab testing, beta acceptance testing and contract negotiations to sell the new gizmo. And the customer was a telecom company that wasn't sure what it would actually be doing three years down the road.

I got tired of shining my crystal ball. My managers got tired of my pushing them to succeed. They wanted me to tell them what they wanted to hear. Hang in there. Soon it will be like the good old days.

But it wasn't going to be like the old days. We were no longer the kids of the '90s technology boom. We were dads and moms trying to keep our tech babies fed during a severe economic downturn. Pressure from our customers to deliver cheaper but technologically more elegant products was intense. We were on the hard edge of survival.

Because our company had been good at generating cash, we had a war chest. We acquired two companies. Even with the new product lines of these acquisitions, our old lines were shrinking. Employee layoffs were part of the picture.

The business came to define me. I wasn't a person. I had been assimilated into my company. I had no outside interests. My life became an endless twilight zone of two-thumbed entries into a hand-held device and sitting in the car in the driveway for an hour, talking on a cell phone.

I had no time for my wife. She was left alone all day to do charity work and provide care for her dying parents while I slew high-tech dragons. I began to realize that her work held a whole lot more meaning than mine seemed to. And I missed her.

My Dad had his first bypass operation at age 37 and died at 57. Even if I dedicated myself to eating alfalfa sprouts at every meal, which I didn't, and working out for three hours a day, which I couldn't, I needed to reduce my stress level.

The pleasant experience of an endoscopy resulting in a prescription for "the little purple pill" confirmed my precarious situation. If stress-induced acid was the start, heart problems couldn't be far behind.

Then I bumped into a college classmate. His experience had been similar to mine. He'd founded and run a software company. Then he sold it. After he sold, he worked for a venture capitalist for a while, but the stress didn't abate. So he decided to change. He checked out of the high-tech start-up venture capital world; he became a college professor.

That sounded like a plan. So now, a few days a week I teach entrepreneurism to wide-eyed liberal arts college students looking to make their way in the big, wide world. I do a little investing in small private companies. I sit on a couple of company boards. I volunteer at charities I admire.

But the change has been damned difficult. I've had to break a 16-year adrenaline habit and redefine myself. My

former No. 2 at the tech company, who left the business about five years ago, put it best. "I'm finally the person I was before I joined that crazy business," he said.

I still miss it. I miss the big orders coming over the fax machine. I miss the meetings. I miss showing off new products at the annual trade shows. I miss some of the people. Hell, I even miss the customers.

I know that I tried my hardest. I know that I never gave up. I believe that I did the best that I could with the equipment God gave me. I tried to be fair with people. If I was hard on them, I did it for the good of the company and its stakeholders. I would do nothing different nor trade any moment.

And now? I don't get stressed out anywhere near as often. I don't feel anxious. I can sleep. Best of all, I spend a lot more time with my wife. Oh, and with our big, clueless black and yellow Labs, Shannon and Cara.

Sometimes I worry that I'm getting dumber, even though I've probably read more in the last 18 months than I did in the previous 10 years. I also seem to be late more often and I lose track of things.

Recently I popped a DVD of the 1988 Michael Keaton movie, *Clean and Sober,* into my player. While I've never suffered from substance abuse, I understand now that defining myself by my company's quarterly earnings reports was an addiction.

Keaton's character, Daryl, is being treated by a drug counselor, played by Morgan Freeman. "The best way to break old habits," the counselor advises Daryl, "is to make new ones."

Now I read the local sports page first rather than *The Wall Street Journal.* I watch MSNBC's *Morning Joe* instead of CNBC's *Squawk Box.* I've recently found myself forgetting when the financial quarters end.

I've made new habits.

Daryl's is a story of redemption amid life's fragility. He ends up a winner because, after his rehabilitation, everyone likes him a whole lot better.

I can't speak for my family and friends, but I can tell you this. After I kicked my habit, I like myself a whole lot better, too.

CREATURES GREAT
AND SMALL

His registered AKC (American Kennel Club) name was "Lt. Bill France of Utah Beach." My wife Jane and I named him after her late father, Bill France, Jr., who landed on Utah Beach during the D-Day invasion of Normandy in World War II.

"Bill" was a strapping black English Labrador retriever, his line known for big square heads, massive chests and short, powerful legs. In an Alabama drawl his veterinarian, Dr. Ted, always called him "Big Man."

"Hey, Big Man," Dr. Ted would say. "How you feelin' today?"

Alanine Transaminase

When Dr. Ted noticed in a routine blood test during Bill's regular visit to the Wexford Veterinary Hospital that Bill's ALT readings were high, he didn't seem alarmed. Alanine transaminase (ALT) is an enzyme found in highest concentrations in the liver; injury to the liver results in release of ALT into the bloodstream.

The higher-than-normal ALT level could be the result of an event as simple as Bill eating something he found in the back yard that didn't agree with him. However, the high reading could also be a sign of a serious liver disease, like hepatitis. Dr. Ted recommended we have Bill's blood retested in a few months.

Sure enough, 90 days later, Dr. Ted found that Bill's ALT level was even higher. An ultrasound of his liver didn't look quite right. Dr. Ted recommended a liver biopsy and referred us to a special veterinary hospital for really sick animals. We were about to discover that veterinary medicine in Pittsburgh is light years beyond the world of English country animal doctor James Herriott's memoir, *All Creatures Great and Small.*

A World-Class Hospital for Dogs

When Jane and I entered the Pittsburgh Veterinary Specialty & Emergency Center (PVSEC), we felt as if we had stepped into an amazingly advanced medical facility. In addition to 24-hour emergency medicine, the PVSEC also provides surgical, internal medicine, critical care, dentistry, dermatology, oncology, neurology and ophthalmology treatment. MRI and CT imaging are available.

Our first consultation was with Dr. Jon, the surgeon who would perform Bill's laparoscopic liver biopsy. The surgery went easily and Bill was walking around like his old self within a week.

Dr. Jon said that Bill's liver "looked boring in a good way." While there was some evidence of tissue scarring, the right medication and diet could manage the condition.

Unfortunately, a short time later, Bill stopped eating. He was admitted to the PVSEC for what we thought would be a brief hospital stay for fluids and medication under the treatment of a warm and caring vet, Dr. Tracey.

In three days things went from bad to worse. Despite another ultrasound and treatment with steroids, Lt. Bill France of Utah Beach was losing his battle. His liver began to fail.

Four days after entering PVSEC, Bill was wheeled into the goodbye room on a gurney. The room was brightly lit. On a table stood a little framed poem about passages next to a book where one could record one's thoughts. I could see the syringes in Dr. Tracey's lab coat pocket as she entered. When she smiled at us, I saw a tear in her eye.

Bill had never argued with us nor done an unkind thing. His sole mission was making us happy. He lifted his head as we cried and told him he was a good boy. We could see he was telling us it was time for him to lie down. He was gone with one push. It seemed our world would never be quite the same.

We were comforted in the knowledge that Dr. Ted, Dr. Jon and Dr. Tracey did everything in their power to make Bill well again. And we know that we would not have wanted him treated anywhere else because of the broad expertise of the vets at PVSEC and the technology at their disposal.

Time passed. One day Jane and I visited an English Lab breeder in Ohio. We'd been thinking about getting a yellow female puppy. But I guess we're gluttons for punishment. We got two, one black, one yellow.

Jane's named them Shannon and Cara. And they've captured our hearts. Just like the Big Man.

BILLIONAIRES FOR A WEEK

Thanks to a computer glitch, I experienced what it felt like to be a billionaire—for a glorious few days.

Last summer my wife called to me from her office, "You've got to see this!" When I looked at our online brokerage account on her computer screen, the balance was $2.2 billion. Now, we've enjoyed some success with our investments, but nothing has hit with that many zeroes.

With the glitch we were still $12 billion lighter than Mark Zuckerberg's Facebook net worth, but at least our multiple had a "b," just like his.

We laughed, then began to muse about all the things that we'd do with the money. Our first inclination was to buy the Pittsburgh Penguins from Ron Burkle. We're season ticket holders, and we actually saw the Pens' 2009 Game 7 triumph at the Joe in Detroit. But Burkle's worth is about $3.2 billion, so he wouldn't need our money.

We thought the computer error would go away by the next day, but it didn't. The balance of $2.2 billion kept showing for almost a week. This was starting to feel palpable.

I looked at my wife and said, "You don't think..."

So we called our investment guys and asked them if they had put money into some incredibly dynamic emerging company and forgot to tell us. We e-mailed them the link to our online investment account so they wouldn't think this was a joke. Their response was, "Just don't show it to your alma maters," where a good many of our charitable dollars are directed in the form of scholarships for less fortunate kids.

Scholarships are usually set up in endowment funds. Colleges and universities typically use four percent of the money, so that it will last forever. They figure the average growth of a portfolio per annum is seven percent, minus three percent for inflation. That's how they arrive at four percent. If we gave them, let's say, a modest $1 billion from our glitch-created assets, each of our institutions could spend about $20 million a year in tuition assistance. With our money, pretty much any kid who wanted to go to our colleges wouldn't need to pay tuition.

Now that sounded cool.

How about our other favorite charity, the local cancer center? A modest $500 million gift could buy a lot of microscopes and petri dishes. We wondered about all the cancer patients who could be helped.

Alas, after a few days, the glitch was fixed and our $2.2 billion disappeared into the ether.

While we enjoyed our few days of rare air, we didn't consider the unhappy lives of lottery winners, who lose their friends due to the green eyes of jealousy. We also overlooked the daily pressure that Mark Zuckerberg endures as he tries to meet the overblown expectations set by investment bankers and the 24-hour financial news cycle. Not to mention the fact that nearly everyone is irritated by Zuckerberg's wealth and demeanor. "Don't you just want to smack him?" Donny Duetsch, who made a fortune himself in advertising, recently asked.

Who among us really wants to be the guy on the receiving end of all that *schadenfreude*? In the interest of full disclosure, shouldn't we all admit that we'd like to see the value of a certain social media stock drop to a buck a share?

Of course, we could all grow up and resign ourselves to the reality that some people just get lucky. As Robert Heinlein said, "Jealousy is invariably the symptom of neurotic insecurity."

Farewell, sweet billions. Farewell!

www.ingramcontent.com/pod-product-compliance
Lightning Source LLC
Chambersburg PA
CBHW071120210326
41519CB00020B/6361